GW00359321

Yearbook 1996

Yearbook 1996

PAINTINGS FROM

THE ULSTER MUSEUM

Looking East Towards the Castlereagh Hills from Malone, Arthur James Ward's Cottage in the foreground by George Trobridge (1856-1909)

List of Illustrations

List of Illustrations

List of Illustrations

January

MONDAY	1	THURSDAY	4
New Year's Day			
TUESDAY	2	FRIDAY	5
WEDNESDAY	3	SATURDAY/SUNDAY	6/7

FARM IN WINTER *c.* 1966: *Tony O'Malley* (born Callan, Co Kilkenny 1913). *Gouache and acrylic on newsprint.*

The artist wrote in 1978: "This was painted from drawings made in previous months around the Cornish coast and from earlier drawings of coastal farms in the County Wexford. My experience of such farmsteads enabled me to express in this gouache the winter atmosphere and the huddle of the farm buildings under the hill with the stormy sea's horizon as a backdrop." Official recognition in Ireland for O'Malley's work did not come until 1975, but he is now one of the most revered of Irish painters. He now spends part of the year in the Bahamas and part in Cornwall and Ireland.

MONDAY	**8**	THURSDAY	**11**
TUESDAY	**9**	FRIDAY	**12**
WEDNESDAY	**10**	SATURDAY/SUNDAY	**13 / 14**

THE SPANISH WALK: *Edwin Morrow* (born Belfast 1877). *Oil on panel.*

Edwin Morrow was one of eight sons of George Morrow, a Belfast painter and decorator. Edwin and four of his brothers studied art and became painters or illustrators: Albert (1863–1927), George (1869–1955), Jack (1872–1926), Edwin himself, and finally Norman, who died young. George Morrow, the best-known, became art editor of Punch *1932–37. This is one of a group of small west of Ireland scenes on panel, which belonged to the Belfast actor Michael Duffy, two of which were bought from him by the Museum in 1972. The Spanish Walk is a street in Galway city.*

MONDAY   **15**   THURSDAY   **18**

TUESDAY   **16**   FRIDAY   **19**

WEDNESDAY   **17**   SATURDAY/SUNDAY   **20 / 21**

AVOCA BRIDGE, CO WICKLOW *c.* 1927: *George William Bissill* (born Fairford, Gloucestershire 1896; died Ashmansworth, near Newbury 1974). *Oil on canvas.*

The son of a coalminer, Bissill himself worked in the mines for six years. He served in France in World War I and was gassed. After the war he studied for one year at Nottingham School of Art, and later worked as a pavement artist in London. In 1924 the Redfern Gallery gave him his first one-man exhibition. He *also exhibited with the Leicester Gallery and the London Group. This Irish view was bought from the Redfern Gallery in 1932 with money from the Lloyd Patterson fund.*

W.P.French. 93

MONDAY	**22**	THURSDAY	**25**
TUESDAY	**23**	FRIDAY	**26**
WEDNESDAY	**24**	SATURDAY/SUNDAY	**27 / 28**

UNTITLED: *Percy French* (born Cloonyquin, Co Roscommon 1854; died Formby, Lancashire 1920). *Watercolour on paper.*

Primarily and popularly known as an entertainer and writer of comic and sentimental songs, Percy French was also a watercolour painter of pleasant but somewhat limited talent. The son of a landowner, he was educated at Windermere College and Foyle College, and then attended Trinity College, Dublin, where he qualified as an engineer. As a student, he discovered his gifts for playing the banjo, composing comic songs and making lightning sketches. This is a typical example of his style, and was part of a presentation album.

MONDAY	29	THURSDAY	1
TUESDAY	30	FRIDAY	2
WEDNESDAY	31	SATURDAY/SUNDAY	3 / 4

DUBLIN STREET SCENE: *Edward Burra* (born South Kensington, London 1905; died Rye, Sussex 1976). *Watercolour and bodycolour over pencil on white laminated board.*

The fact that Burra's health was always delicate has been taken to explain why he worked largely in watercolour instead of oil, and why he spent most of his life working in seclusion at the family home near Rye. However, in spite of his weak constitution, he travelled a great deal in Europe, the United States and *Mexico, in search of the seamy street life which fascinated him. His large watercolours took on a grotesque quality reminiscent of James Ensor or George Grosz. Burra visited Ireland several times about 1948, and painted a series of 12 or 15 Irish scenes, which were exhibited at the Leicester Galleries in London the following year. The material he found in Ireland re-invigorated his painting, which had stagnated since about 1942.*

MONDAY	5	THURSDAY	8
TUESDAY	6	FRIDAY	9
WEDNESDAY	7	SATURDAY/SUNDAY	10 / 11

COAL QUAY, EARLY MORNING: *Colin Middleton* (born Belfast 1910; died Bangor, Co Down 1983). *Oil on canvas.*

During the 1930s Middleton followed with interest the work of Paul Nash, Tristam Hillier and Edward Wadsworth. On discovering the work of Salvador Dali he described himself as "the only surrealist painter working in Ireland". He never abandoned the practice of sober objective streetscape painting such as this, and throughout his career was in the habit of working in five or six apparently unrelated styles at the same time. Middleton taught part-time at the Belfast College of Art and later, in 1955, full-time at Coleraine Technical College. From 1961 to 1970 he was head of the art department of Friends' School, Lisburn.

MONDAY	**12**	THURSDAY	**15**
TUESDAY	**13**	FRIDAY	**16**
WEDNESDAY	**14**	SATURDAY/SUNDAY	**17 / 18**

CHILDREN PLAYING ON THE LAGAN: *Gerard Dillon*

(born Belfast 1916; died Dublin 1971). *Oil on board.*

From 1934 to 1939 Dillon worked for a decorating firm in London. About 1936 he began painting seriously, visiting Connemara frequently. He spent the war years in Belfast and Dublin, and was associated with exhibitions with George Campbell, Dan O'Neill and Neville Johnston. From 1943 he was a regular contributor and committee member of the Irish Exhibition of Living Art. Dillon's subject matter revolves around his own experiences growing up in the Falls Road area of Belfast, in working class terraced houses. This early painting shares its subject with much of the work of William Conor.

MONDAY 19   THURSDAY 22

TUESDAY 20   FRIDAY 23

WEDNESDAY 21   SATURDAY/SUNDAY 24 / 25

MOURNE FOOTHILLS: *Tom Carr* (born Belfast 1909). *Watercolour on white wove paper.*

Probably painted shortly before Carr's exhibition at George McClelland's Galleries in Belfast in 1973, this is an example of Carr's later, very liquid watercolours, which are far removed from Euston Road conventions, and close in style to the work of T P Flanagan. Carr was a much less intellectually analytic painter than the orthodox Euston Roaders like William Coldstream, Claude Rogers, Graham Bell or Lawrence Gowing, and less dogmatic than the Objective Abstractionists to whom he had previously been attached. Tom Carr is an academician of the Royal Ulster Academy, and the only Northern Ireland member of the Royal Society of Painters in Watercolour.

MONDAY	26	THURSDAY	29
TUESDAY	27	FRIDAY	1
WEDNESDAY	28	SATURDAY/SUNDAY	2 / 3

CLADDAGH DUFF, CONNEMARA *c.* 1950-1: *George Campbell* (born Arklow, Co Wicklow 1917; died Dublin 1979). *Oil on masonite.*

George Campbell, son of the primitive painter Gretta Bowen, and younger brother of Arthur Campbell, attended Richview School, Dublin, before the family moved to Belfast. He left commercial work to become a full-time painter, a craft at which he was practically self-taught. This painting was presented to the Ulster Museum by the Thomas Haverty Trust in 1957. Claddagh Duff is a village in the most westerly part of Connemara. The artist wrote, "I painted it because I liked the build-up of textures and shapes; it is difficult to say precisely but the whole thing is a nice unit."

MONDAY	4	THURSDAY	7
TUESDAY	5	FRIDAY	8
WEDNESDAY	6	SATURDAY/SUNDAY	9 / 10

LISCANNOR: *Grace Henry* (born Peterhead, Aberdeenshire 1868; died Dublin 1953). *Oil on wood.*

Like her husband, Paul Henry, Grace Mitchell was a child of the manse, though her family was very well off. She studied art in Brussels and Paris, where she met and married Paul Henry in 1903. After living in Surrey, they paid a visit to Achill Island, Co Mayo, in 1912 and stayed for eight years. Following this they settled in Merrion Row, Dublin, founding the Dublin Painters Society in 1920. While Paul Henry became perhaps the representative Irish landscape painter, Grace Henry's development was more tortuous, veering between near abstraction and sensitive renditions of local atmosphere. The Henrys eventually separated, though they did not divorce, and Grace Henry was elected an honorary RHA at the age of eighty-one.

MONDAY **11**

TUESDAY **12**

WEDNESDAY **13**

THURSDAY **14**

FRIDAY **15**

SATURDAY/SUNDAY **16 / 17**
St Patrick's Day

SCENE IN COUNTY WICKLOW *c.* 1820: *James Arthur O'Connor* (born Dublin 1792; died London 1841). *Oil on canvas.*

After 1822, James Arthur O'Connor settled in London and exhibited at the Royal Academy and the British Institution. This is an idealised view of the Wicklow countryside in the tradition of classical landscape painting. The Great Sugar Loaf and Little Sugar Loaf mountains are Italianised in treatment in the manner of the great seventeenth century painter Claude Lorraine. The classical formula of blue distance, green middle ground and brown foreground is observed. Later on O'Connor's landscapes became much more gloomy and melancholic in accord with contemporary tastes for the sublime or romantic.

MONDAY **18**

TUESDAY **19**

WEDNESDAY **20**

THURSDAY **21**

FRIDAY **22**

SATURDAY/SUNDAY **23 / 24**

ONE ROOM *c.* 1954: *Anne Yeats* (born Dublin 1919).
Oil on canvas.

Anne Yeats is the daughter of the poet W B Yeats and his wife George Hyde-Lees, and therefore grand-daughter of John Butler Yeats and niece of Jack Butler Yeats the renowned artists. Anne studied at the Royal Hibernian Academy Schools from 1933 to 1936, and was sometime a pupil of Lilian Davidson. From 1940 to 1946 she worked as a freelance stage designer, but in 1941 she started to paint, and held her first one-woman exhibition in Dublin in 1946. Anne Yeats's work is preoccupied with the human situation, particularly with the isolation of the individual. In the 1940s she worked mainly in watercolour and gouache, often incorporating wax with watercolour. However uncertainty about the permanence of the wax led her to abandon the method, and her later work is mainly in oil.

March *1996*

MONDAY	25	THURSDAY	28
TUESDAY	26	FRIDAY	29
WEDNESDAY	27	SATURDAY/SUNDAY	30 / 31

GLENOE: *Gerard Dillon* (born Belfast 1916; died Dublin 1971). *Oil on board.*

Glenoe is a picturesque and much-painted small village near Larne, Co Antrim, just inland from Larne Lough. The Ulster Museum has views of it by Andrew Nicholl and other earlier painters. Straightforward landscape subjects are not usually associated with Gerard Dillon, but this is an exception. Dillon visited Italy in 1947 and Spain about 1952. From 1958 he figured in international exhibitions in America, Rome and London, and toured Denmark and the USA. He went to live in Dublin in 1968, and died three years later in the Adelaide Hospital. He was buried in Belfast.

MONDAY 1

THURSDAY 4

TUESDAY 2

FRIDAY 5
Good Friday

WEDNESDAY 3

SATURDAY/SUNDAY 6/7
Easter Sunday

FERRY BOATS, RIVER LAGAN: *William Conor* (born Belfast 1881; died Belfast 1968). *Watercolour over pencil, with surface scraping, on white paper.*

This was painted between about 1925 and 1928, and is a pleasingly sombre scene on the River Lagan near the Belfast docks. Conor was the first Irish member of the Royal Institute of Oil Painters (ROI). He exhibited at the Royal Academy, the Royal Portrait Society and the Society of Portrait Painters. He was elected ARHA in 1938 and RHA in 1946. From 1957 to 1964 he was President of the Royal Ulster Academy. He received an honorary MA from the Queen's University of Belfast in 1957, and was awarded a Civil List Pension in 1959. He died at his house in Salisbury Avenue and was buried in Carnmoney Churchyard.

| MONDAY | 8 | THURSDAY | 11 |
| Easter Monday | | | |

| TUESDAY | 9 | FRIDAY | 12 |

| WEDNESDAY | 10 | SATURDAY/SUNDAY | 13 / 14 |

TORY ISLAND FROM TOR MOR *c.* 1958: *Derek Hill*
(born England 1916). *Oil on canvas.*

After a distinguished international career as a stage designer and portrait painter, Derek Hill based himself in north Donegal and first visited Tory Island in 1954. He has always loved islands, the more remote the better – St Kilda, Fair Isle, Foula. Tor More is a towering outcrop of rock at the extreme eastern end of Tory Island. Derek Hill has presented his house and collection (the Glebe Gallery, Churchill, Co Donegal) to the Irish State, and it is now open to the public.

MONDAY	15	THURSDAY	18
TUESDAY	16	FRIDAY	19
WEDNESDAY	17	SATURDAY/SUNDAY	20 / 21

FLOWERS ON A SHORE: *Dan O'Neill* (born Belfast 1920; died Belfast 1974). *Oil on canvas.*

Dan O'Neill is associated with George Campbell and Gerard Dillon as one of the trio of imaginative Belfast painters who were made famous by the Dublin dealer Victor Waddington in the 1940s. The son of an electrician, O'Neill followed his father's trade and worked in the shipyards before becoming a full-time artist in 1946. He had little formal training beyond a short spell at the Belfast School of Art and a period as a studio assistant to Sidney Smith. O'Neill's work has an uncannily surrealist quality, of which this strange still life is a splendid example.

MONDAY	22	THURSDAY	25
TUESDAY	23	FRIDAY	26
WEDNESDAY	24	SATURDAY/SUNDAY	27 / 28

BEWLEY'S RESTAURANT II *c.* 1980: *Hector McDonnell* (born 1947). *Oil on canvas.*

One of the McDonnell family of Glenarm Castle, Co Antrim, Hector McDonnell has acquired an international reputation for his painting. The Bewley's restaurant featured here is the well-known establishment in Grafton Street, Dublin. In this large painting, McDonnell has treated the dark interior with light penetrating the windows in the face of the viewer in a novel way, which recalls the paintings of the "Glasgow Boys" at the turn of the century.

MONDAY 29

THURSDAY 2

TUESDAY 30

FRIDAY 3

WEDNESDAY 1

SATURDAY/SUNDAY 4 / 5

ROSTREVOR: *Andrew Nicholl* (born Belfast 1804; died London 1886). *Watercolour on white paper.*

At about the age of eighteen Andrew Nicholl was apprenticed as a compositor with the Belfast printer Francis Dalzell Finlay, who in 1824 started the newspaper The Northern Whig, *and who spotted Nicholl's talent as a draughtsman. This Co. Down scene follows on from the series of 101 views of the Antrim Coast which are Nicholl's earliest dateable work, two of them being dated 1828. He would have then been about twenty-four, and was still an apprentice to Finlay in Belfast. His early style is one of clean crisp washes rather like John Varley, and was probably derived from looking at aquatint illustrations in travel books.*

MONDAY 6

THURSDAY 9

TUESDAY 7

FRIDAY 10

WEDNESDAY 8

SATURDAY/SUNDAY 11 / 12

LEENANE *c.* 1913: *Paul Henry* (born Belfast 1876; died Bray, Co Wicklow 1958). *Oil on board.*

One of the most successful painters to have come from Belfast, Paul Henry was educated at the Methodist College and the Royal Belfast Academical Institution. About the age of fifteen, he received painting lessons from Thomas Bond Walker. Between 1900 and 1912 Paul Henry lived mostly in London, and was much influenced by Whistler and the post-impressionists. In 1910 he first visited Achill Island, Co Mayo, which was to become his favourite painting ground. This little panel was given to the Belfast Museum and Art Gallery by Dr R I Best through the Friends of the National Collections of Ireland, in 1959.

MONDAY 13 THURSDAY 16

TUESDAY 14 FRIDAY 17

WEDNESDAY 15 SATURDAY/SUNDAY 18 / 19

FIVE TREES BY A RIVER: *Hans Iten* (born Zurich 1874; died Bulach, Switzerland 1930). *Oil on board.*

This Swiss artist spent most of his working life in Belfast. He studied at the art school in St Gall, and then in Paris where it appears he became friendly with the painter Pierre Montèzin. In 1904 he came to Belfast as a damask designer with the linen firm of McCrum, Watson and Mercer in Linenhall Street, and during this time he lived at 18 South Parade, Ormeau Road.

This little panel, which may well have been painted on the banks of the Lagan, is a good example of Iten's broad impressionistic style.

MONDAY	**20**	THURSDAY	**23**
TUESDAY	**21**	FRIDAY	**24**
WEDNESDAY	**22**	SATURDAY/SUNDAY	**25 / 26**

LINER ON STOCKS: *Sir Robert Ponsonby Staples*, 12th Baronet (born Dundee, Scotland 1853; succeeded to the baronetcy 1933; died 1943). *Oil on canvas.*

This is the central panel of a triptych entitled Shipbuilding in Belfast, *which Staples began in 1904 and laboured on for two years. The two pendant panels are called* Turbine Makers *and* The Bangor Boat. *In November 1906, Staples offered it to the new Belfast City Hall, completed that year, and a public subscription was launched to pay for it. However, it eventually came into the possession of Mr David Waugh, who sold it to the Museum in 1913. Staples was disappointed as he wished it to be framed to his specification as a triptych and not in three separate frames. Some irate correspondence remains in the Museum's files. The Museum also owns a large number of sketches for these three compositions.*

MONDAY   27   THURSDAY   30

TUESDAY   28   FRIDAY   31

WEDNESDAY   29   SATURDAY/SUNDAY   1 / 2

EAGLE'S NEST, KILLARNEY: *William Sadler II* (active in Dublin from *c.* 1782; died Dublin 1839). *Oil on panel.*

This William Sadler was the second of a dynasty of three Dublin landscape painters of the same name – father, son and grandson. He was the teacher of the painter James Arthur O'Connor, and his paintings are usually on small mahogany panels. By the beginning of the nineteenth century, the lakes of Killarney had become an established tourist attraction for *visitors to Ireland. The Eagle's Nest, a mountain between the Upper and Lower Lakes, had a famous echo which was demonstrated to tourists, as here, by local hirelings blowing bugles and firing cannon.*

June *1996*

MONDAY	3	THURSDAY	6
TUESDAY	4	FRIDAY	7
WEDNESDAY	5	SATURDAY/SUNDAY	8 / 9

NASTURTIUMS: *Mildred Anne Butler* (born Kilmurry, Thomastown, Co Kilkenny 1858; died Kilmurry 1941). *Watercolour on paper.*

Mildred Butler was the daughter of Captain Henry Butler of Kilmurry, a grandson of the eleventh Viscount Mountgarret. She studied at the Westminster School of Art, and privately with Paul Naftel and the cattle painter Frank Calderon. In Cornwall she worked with Norman Garstin, and was associated with the Newlyn School. As well as exhibiting in London and Dublin, she exhibited regularly at the Belfast Art Society, which, on becoming the Ulster Academy of Arts in 1930, elected her as one of its first academicians. This typical Mildred Butler sketch comes from an album of watercolours presented to one of the early active members of the Belfast Art Society, Sidney Mary Thompson, who married the Swiss artist Rodolphe Christen.

MONDAY **10**   THURSDAY **13**

TUESDAY **11**   FRIDAY **14**

WEDNESDAY **12**   SATURDAY/SUNDAY **15 / 16**

AFTER MILKING TIME: *James Stoupe* (born Belfast 1872; died Belfast 1949). *Oil on board.*

The son of a carpenter, James (sometimes called Séamus) Stoupe was educated at the Belfast Model School and possibly the Belfast Government School of Design under George Trobridge. From 1904 to 1938 he was modelling master at the Belfast School of Art. He was elected a member of the Belfast Art Society in 1894, and in 1921 was President of the Ulster Arts Club, which owns his bronze of William Gray. Mainly known as a sculptor, Stoupe also practiced painting and lithography. The Ulster Museum also has an oil study for this painting.

MONDAY	**17**	THURSDAY	**20**
TUESDAY	**18**	FRIDAY	**21**
WEDNESDAY	**19**	SATURDAY/SUNDAY	**22 / 23**

THREE FRIENDS *c.* 1970: ***Dan O'Neill*** (born Belfast 1920; died 1974). *Oil on panel.*

Dan O'Neill had hardly any formal training as a painter and until 1944 he worked as an electrical engineer in the Belfast shipyards and painted only in his spare time. He then received encouragement from collectors and critics in Belfast and Dublin, and was given one-man shows by Victor Waddington's gallery. He is often associated with two other primitive artists, Gerard *Dillon and George Campbell. This is one of three late paintings exhibited in 1970 and painted perhaps one year previously.*

MONDAY	24	THURSDAY	27
TUESDAY	25	FRIDAY	28
WEDNESDAY	26	SATURDAY/SUNDAY	29 / 30

WICKLOW LANDSCAPE: *Paul Henry* (born Belfast 1876; died Bray, Co Wicklow 1958).   *Oil on board.*

The Henrys lived at Carigoona Cottage, near Enniskerry, Co Wicklow, from 1930 to 1951. Paul Henry suffered all his life, probably unknowingly, from red-green colour blindness, and after a nervous breakdown in 1945 became almost totally blind. He and his wife Grace, a fellow artist, moved to Bray in 1951. The couple later separated, though they did not divorce. Grace *Henry died in 1953, and Paul then married Mabel Young, who died in 1974.*

MONDAY	1	THURSDAY	4
TUESDAY	2	FRIDAY	5
WEDNESDAY	3	SATURDAY/SUNDAY	6/7

TWILIGHT, MOYADD *c.* 1952: *Tom Carr* (born Belfast 1909). *Oil on canvas.*

Tom Carr as a boy received some lessons from the Swiss painter Hans Iten who settled in Belfast. Later, at Oundle School, Northamptonshire, he was taught by the art master, the Belfast-born E M O'Rorke Dickey. In London, Carr was associated first with the Objective Abstractionists, and then with the Euston Road School (other members being William Coldstream, Victor Pasmore, Graham Bell and Claude Rogers). By the outbreak of the Second World War he had returned to Ulster, and settled with his wife and family at Newcastle, Co Down. This evocative evening landscape of the Mourne countryside dates from this period.

MONDAY	**8**	THURSDAY	**11**
TUESDAY	**9**	FRIDAY	**12**
WEDNESDAY	**10**	SATURDAY/SUNDAY	**13 / 14**

MILL NEAR BEGGAR'S BUSH, CO DUBLIN *c.* 1813:
Francis Danby (born Wexford 1793; died Exmouth 1861).
Watercolour on white wove paper.

Francis Danby left Ireland permanently in 1813, settling in Bristol. This is one of four small watercolours which represent his early Irish work, which is very rare. Ringsend and Beggar's Bush are now suburbs of Dublin, south of where the River Liffey enters Dublin Bay and where it is joined by the River Dodder. According to a local historian, Mr Danny Parkinson of Donnybrook, the site of this flour mill can be found opposite the present entrance to Landsdowne Road rugby ground.

| MONDAY | 15 | THURSDAY | 18 |

| TUESDAY | 16 | FRIDAY | 19 |

| WEDNESDAY | 17 | SATURDAY/SUNDAY | 20 / 21 |

A BANK OF FLOWERS, WITH A VIEW OF BRAY, CO. WICKLOW: *c.* 1835: *Andrew Nicholl* (born Belfast 1804; died London 1886). *Watercolour on white paper.*

During the second half of the 1830s Andrew Nicholl lived for some time in Dublin, where he appears to have conceived his most attractive compositions, these distant views seen through a bank of wild flowers. This one is actually inscribed on the back: "Summer wild flowers: Bray and the Valley of the Dargle from Killiney Hill, Co. Dublin". The delicate white sprays of cow-parsley are drawn with the tip of a sharp knife, scraping away the darker paint and exposing the white paper beneath. Other similar Irish views are known, including Derry, Carrickfergus and the White Rocks at Portrush.

MONDAY	22	THURSDAY	25
TUESDAY	23	FRIDAY	26
WEDNESDAY	24	SATURDAY/SUNDAY	27 / 28

APPLE ORCHARD WITH CABBAGES: *Samuel McCloy* (born Lisburn, Co Antrim 1831; died Balham, London 1904). *Watercolour over pencil on white paper.*

The youngest of five children of a Lisburn painter and glazier, Samuel McCloy was apprenticed to the Belfast engraving firm of J & T Smith before studying at the Belfast Government School of Design 1850-51. Here he won several prizes and an exhibition which took him to the Training School for Masters in South Kensington. In 1854 he was appointed Master of the Waterford School of Art. McCloy possessed a sure control of pure watercolour and a real feeling for plant life. It is likely, however, that he would have regarded these watercolours merely as studies for backgrounds in his genre paintings. His oil paintings, saleable essays in bourgeois sentimentalism, never approach this vitality.

MONDAY	29	THURSDAY	1
TUESDAY	30	FRIDAY	2
WEDNESDAY	31	SATURDAY/SUNDAY	3 / 4

THE YELLOW BUNGALOW: *Gerard Dillon* (born Belfast 1916; died Dublin 1971). *Oil on canvas.*

Dillon was one of the most imaginative of the folk-inspired Irish painters of the twentieth century. He was born in Lower Clonard Street, off the Falls Road, the youngest of eight children of a postman. Leaving school at the age of fourteen, he worked as a house-painter and though enrolled by his mother for evening classes at the Belfast College of Art did not attend.

From 1934 to 1939 he worked for a decorating firm in London. About 1936 he began painting seriously, visiting Connemara frequently. This picture was painted in a bungalow at Roundstone, Co Galway.

MONDAY	5	THURSDAY	8
TUESDAY	6	FRIDAY	9
WEDNESDAY	7	SATURDAY/SUNDAY	10 / 11

BUNDORAN SANDS, STORMY DAY: *Nathaniel Hone* (born Dublin 1831; died Malahide, Co Dublin 1917). *Oil on board.*

One of a family dynasty of painters which included Nathaniel Hone the Elder, his son Horace Hone the miniature painter, and, in the present century, the stained glass artist Evie Hone, Nathaniel Hone the Younger was one of the best Irish landscape painters of the nineteenth century. This tiny oil sketch shows a Donegal scene, evidently painted "on-the-spot". Trained in Paris, Hone learned this spontaneous sketching style in both oil and watercolour through his long association with the Barbizon painters in France.

MONDAY	12	THURSDAY	15
TUESDAY	13	FRIDAY	16
WEDNESDAY	14	SATURDAY/SUNDAY	17 / 18

THE FOUR COURTS, DUBLIN *c.* 1940: *Norah McGuinness* (born Londonderry 1903; died Dublin 1980). *Gouache on heavy white paper.*

After a short period in New York, where she gained experience in designing window-dressing for a Fifth Avenue store, Norah McGuinness returned to Ireland permanently in 1939, making window displays for the Brown Thomas department store. Her work at this time, mainly landscape and townscape, imitated *the work of the French Fauves of thirty years before. In 1944 she succeeded Mainie Jellet as President of the Irish Exhibition of Living Art. With Nano Reid, she represented Ireland at the Venice Biennale of 1950.*

MONDAY	**19**	THURSDAY	**22**
TUESDAY	**20**	FRIDAY	**23**
WEDNESDAY	**21**	SATURDAY/SUNDAY	**24 / 25**

RUSTICS DANCING OUTSIDE AN INN: *Samson Toogood Roche* (born Youghal, Co Cork 1757/59; died Woodbine Hill, Co Waterford 1847). *Watercolour and bodycolour on thin white card.*

Like so many miniature painters, Roche was born a deaf-mute. On 7 June 1788 he married his first cousin, Miss Roch, only daughter of James Roch of Odell Lodge, Co Waterford, who brought him a handsome fortune. In 1792 he moved to Bath,

where he carried on a successful practice. On his retirement in 1822 he went to live with his relations at Woodbine Hill, and he was buried in the family plot at Ardmore, Co Waterford. This is a fancy subject, the inn and the church in the background evidently imaginary, and the "rustics" very genteel. As might be expected from a painter of miniatures, the strokes are tiny and white bodycolour is used as well as watercolour.

MONDAY	**26**	THURSDAY	**29**
TUESDAY	**27**	FRIDAY	**30**
WEDNESDAY	**28**	SATURDAY/SUNDAY	**31 / 1**

IN THE MOURNES: *John Luke* (born Belfast 1906; died Belfast 1975). *Tempera on panel.*

Born in north Belfast, the son of a fireman, Luke studied at the Belfast School of Art under James Stoupe and Newton Penprase, and in 1927 won a Dunville Scholarship to the Slade School of Art in London. There he studied under Henry Tonks, and for a time shared a studio with F E McWilliam. Luke returned to Belfast in 1931, to live with his parents in Lewis Street. He later became friendly with John Hewitt and William McClughin. He taught life classes in the Belfast School of Art for many years until 1973, and was renowned among the students for exceptional exactitude and strictness. This is a good example of his formalised landscapes using a tempera technique which he developed himself.

MONDAY	2	THURSDAY	5
TUESDAY	3	FRIDAY	6
WEDNESDAY	4	SATURDAY/SUNDAY	7 / 8

LOOKING EAST TOWARDS THE CASTLEREAGH HILLS FROM MALONE, ARTHUR JAMES WARD'S COTTAGE IN THE FOREGROUND: *George Trobridge* (born Crediton, Devon 1856; died Gloucester 1909). *Watercolour over pencil on white wove paper.*

After abandoning an uncongenial office job, Trobridge won a scholarship in 1876 to the National Art Training School at South Kensington, where he showed great talent. In 1880 he was recommended by Sir Edward Poynter for the position of head master of the Belfast School of Art, a post which he held until 1901. Trobridge was a gentle idealist; a Christian Socialist, a strict vegetarian and a teetotaller. His objectively realistic watercolours seem totally unaffected by his interest in Swedenborgian mysticism. This view appears to be taken from the vicinity of his home in Stranmillis, looking across the Lagan valley.

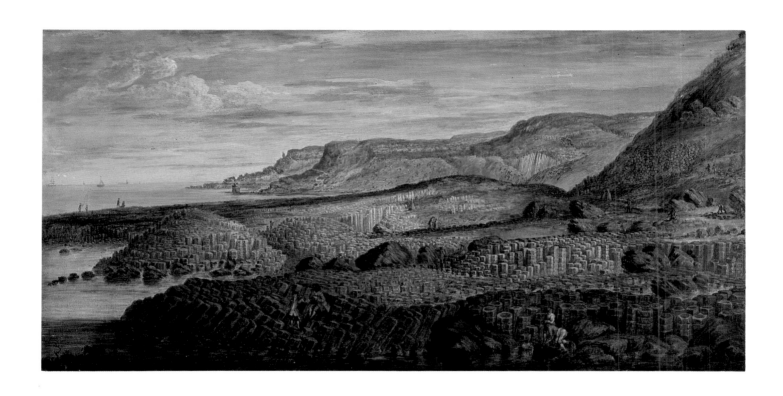

MONDAY **9**	THURSDAY **12**
TUESDAY **10**	FRIDAY **13**
WEDNESDAY **11**	SATURDAY/SUNDAY **14/15**

THE WEST PROSPECT OF THE GIANT'S CAUSEWAY

c. 1739/40: ***Susanna Drury (Mrs Warter)*** (active in Dublin 1733-70). *Gouache on vellum.*

Miss Drury was an obscure but very able painter whose views of the Giant's Causeway (then only recently discovered) are landmarks both in Irish topographical painting and in European scientific illustration. Her pair of perspectives of the Giant's Causeway won the first £25 premium of the Dublin Society in 1740, and were soon afterwards engraved in London by the French Huguenot François Viviarès. These engravings, circulated throughout Europe, provided the great French geologist Nicolas Demarest (1725-1815) with pictorial evidence to support his theory of the volcanic origin of basalt rock.

MONDAY	**16**	THURSDAY	**19**
TUESDAY	**17**	FRIDAY	**20**
WEDNESDAY	**18**	SATURDAY/SUNDAY	**21 / 22**

LANDSCAPE WITH THREE COTTAGES: *Grace Henry*
(born Peterhead, Aberdeenshire 1868; died Dublin 1953).
Oil on board.

Grace Henry had an exhibition at Magee Gallery, Belfast in 1923, and moved to Paris to study under Andre Lhote in 1924-25. Though she separated from her husband Paul Henry during this decade, they were never divorced. It is a mistake to regard Grace Henry's painting as overshadowed by that of her celebrated husband. Her simplified landscapes of Achill Island and Connemara contrasted sharply with the views she painted on the continent, particularly in the South of France and Italy.

MONDAY	23	THURSDAY	26
TUESDAY	24	FRIDAY	27
WEDNESDAY	25	SATURDAY/SUNDAY	28 / 29

SEPTEMBER EVENING, BALLYMOTE *c.* 1951: *Colin Middleton* (born Belfast 1910; died Bangor, Co Down 1983). *Oil on canvas.*

The son of a damask engineer, Colin Middleton attended the Belfast Royal Academy, and in 1927 went into his father's trade. He managed to go to evening classes at the Belfast School of Art to study under Newton Penprase where his fellow students included Romeo Toogood, William Scott and F E McWilliam. On a visit to London in 1928 he was impressed by the work of Van Gogh. This landscape of Co Sligo certainly shows a debt to Van Gogh's expressionistic brushstroke, as well as to the work of Jack Butler Yeats.

MONDAY	30	THURSDAY	3
TUESDAY	1	FRIDAY	4
WEDNESDAY	2	SATURDAY/SUNDAY	5/6

STACKBUILDING: *Samuel McCloy* (born Lisburn, Co Antrim 1831; died Balham, London 1904). *Watercolour over pencil on white paper.*

This small watercolour study, less than the size of a postcard, is more freely painted than most of McCloy's observational work. It is, however, a most disciplined piece of watercolour, the sunlight and shade carefully sorted out, the figures and fence-palings deftly placed. McCloy succeeds in a very small space in suggesting an outdoor event in hot, bright sunshine. McCloy's exhibited work in oil and watercolour belongs to a sentimental genre which carries on the tradition of Mulready. However, his tightly executed watercolour studies of landscape and vegetation accord much more with modern tastes.

MONDAY	7	THURSDAY	10
TUESDAY	8	FRIDAY	11
WEDNESDAY	9	SATURDAY/SUNDAY	12 / 13

UNTITLED: *Jack Butler Yeats* (born London 1871; died Dublin 1957). *Oil on board.*

The most distinguished Irish painter of this century, Jack Yeats was the youngest of five children of the painter John Butler Yeats (1839-1922), and brother of the poet W B Yeats (1865-1939). He was taken to Sligo at the age of eight to live with his mother's parents, the Pollexfens, and much of his imagery was formed there. He was particularly interested in rural horse-racing. This tiny panel recalls the fact that Yeats's early career lay in illustration.

MONDAY	**14**	THURSDAY	**17**
TUESDAY	**15**	FRIDAY	**18**
WEDNESDAY	**16**	SATURDAY/SUNDAY	**19 / 20**

DONKEYS: *Letitia Hamilton* (born Dublin 1878; died 1964). *Oil on canvas.*

A pupil of Sir William Orpen in Dublin, Letitia Hamilton went on to study art in London and in Belgium under Frank Brangwyn. As a young lady of means, she was able to travel widely on the continent, and was influenced by contemporary French artists such as Dufy as well as by Irish painters such as Roderic O'Conor and Paul Henry. Letitia Hamilton's main subjects were Irish landscapes and hunting scenes. She was a founder member of the Dublin Painters Group, and was elected RHA in 1944.

MONDAY **21**   THURSDAY **24**

TUESDAY **22**   FRIDAY **25**

WEDNESDAY **23**   SATURDAY/SUNDAY **26 / 27**

AN IRISH INTERIOR: *Anthony Carey Stannus* (born Carrickfergus 1830; died London 1919). *Watercolour, heightened with white, on white paper.*

An artist of considerable ability, Stannus missed inclusion in Strickland's A Dictionary of Irish Artists, *published in 1913, and for some time has remained obscure. The son of an architect practising in Belfast, he was educated at the Royal Belfast Academical Institution, and was one of the earliest students at* the Belfast School of Design under Claude Lorrain Nursey, 1850-54. Stannus exhibited an Interior of an Irish Cabin at the Royal Hibernian Academy in 1860, priced at £10. He also showed An Irish Cabin (possibly the same picture) at the Royal Academy in 1863. Stannus's obituary in the Belfast Newsletter says that, "His kindly nature and sunny disposition won for him hosts of friends in all parts of the country."

MONDAY	28	THURSDAY	31

TUESDAY	29	FRIDAY	1

WEDNESDAY	30	SATURDAY/SUNDAY	2 / 3

LANDSCAPE WITH CATTLE: *Nathaniel Hone* (born Dublin 1831; died Malahide, Co Dublin 1917). *Oil on canvas.*

Sometimes called Nathaniel Hone the Younger to distinguish him from his eighteenth century namesake and ancestor, Hone started his career as an engineer. At the age of twenty-two he decided to give this up and become a painter. In 1853 he went to Paris and studied under Adolphe Yvon and Thomas Couture. About 1857 he moved to Barbizon, working with Millet, Theodore Rousseau, Charles Jacque and Harpignies, who was a particular friend. He remained at Barbizon for twenty years, occasionally visiting the Mediterranean. Returning to Ireland in 1875, he settled at Malahide, where he farmed. In 1894 he succeeded Sir Thomas Jones as Professor of Painting to the RHA. Hone's widow gave over 500 of his paintings and 887 of his landscape watercolours to the National Galley of Ireland. This little canvas was probably painted near the artist's home in Malahide.

| MONDAY | 4 | THURSDAY | 7 |

| TUESDAY | 5 | FRIDAY | 8 |

| WEDNESDAY | 6 | SATURDAY/SUNDAY | 9 / 10 |

FARMLANDS, DONEGAL: *Hans Iten* (born Zurich 1874; died Bulach, Switzerland 1930). *Oil on canvas.*

One of the best painters working in Belfast during the early twentieth century, Iten was an active member of the Belfast Art Society (the forerunner of the Royal Ulster Academy). In 1911 he made an unsuccessful proposal to bring an exhibition of post-impressionist paintings, then on show in Dublin, to Belfast. In 1924 he lectured on Van Gogh to the Belfast Art Society. He exhibited at the Paris Salon, the Glasgow Institute, the Royal Academy and the Royal Hibernian Academy, and was Vice-President of the Ulster Arts Club. In 1926 he held an exhibition at Rodman's Gallery in Belfast. He always maintained his continental links, visiting Europe regularly, and died while on holiday in Switzerland.

MONDAY	**11**	THURSDAY	**14**
TUESDAY	**12**	FRIDAY	**15**
WEDNESDAY	**13**	SATURDAY/SUNDAY	**16 / 17**

HELIANTHUS: *David Wilson* (born Minterburn, Co Tyrone 1873; died London 1935). *Watercolour on paper.*

Wilson's reputation was principally as a caricaturist and cartoonist, but he was also a very able painter of flowers and landscapes in watercolour. His father was the Presbyterian minister of Minterburn, Co Tyrone, but was later moved to Malone Presbyterian Church, Belfast in 1933. David attended the Royal Belfast Academical Institution and began to work in a bank, but studied drawing at evening classes at the Government School of Design, and soon revealed a gift for caricature. He went to London, where, after some years of struggle, he became a leading Fleet Street black and white illustrator. Wilson was a member of the Royal Society of British Artists and the Royal Institute of Painters in Watercolour. He died in London on 2 January 1935.

MONDAY	**18**	THURSDAY	**21**
TUESDAY	**19**	FRIDAY	**22**
WEDNESDAY	**20**	SATURDAY/SUNDAY	**23 / 24**

A VIEW OF THE RIVER BOYNE *c.* 1757: *Thomas Mitchell*
(born London 1735; died 1790). *Oil on canvas.*

This artist, who also worked as a shipwright to the Admiralty, was working in Ireland in 1757, possibly for the Duke of Devonshire who was Lord Lieutenant 1754-56. His view of the site of the Battle of the Boyne is intended to commemorate and glorify King William III's victory of 1690. We are looking south-east from near Towneley Hall, with the village of Oldbridge on the right. While the obelisk certainly did exist (erected in 1736 and blown up in 1922), the equestrian statue of King William is fanciful. It could be based on the statue by Grinling Gibbons which was set up in College Green, Dublin, in 1701, and blown up in 1929.

MONDAY	**25**	THURSDAY	**28**
TUESDAY	**26**	FRIDAY	**29**
WEDNESDAY	**27**	SATURDAY/SUNDAY	**30 / 1**

GREEN LANDSCAPE: *T P Flanagan* (born Enniskillen, Co Fermanagh 1929). *Oil on board.*

While at school in Enniskillen, T P Flanagan attended evening classes at the Technical College and received lessons from Kathleen Bridle, who also taught William Scott. He went on to study at Belfast College'of Art, 1949-53, then taught art in schools in Lisburn and Ballynahinch, and later at the Belfast College of Art. From 1955 he lectured in art at St Mary's College of Education, Belfast, and was head of the art department there from 1965 until his retirement in 1984. Now one of the foremost painters in Northern Ireland, Flanagan works mostly on landscapes, particularly in Donegal and his native Fermanagh. While his work can look very abstract, it almost invariably contains landscape elements. He often uses oil paint very thinly in the way he uses watercolour.

MONDAY	2	THURSDAY	5
TUESDAY	3	FRIDAY	6
WEDNESDAY	4	SATURDAY/SUNDAY	7/8

STRICKLAND'S GLEN, BANGOR: *Samuel McCloy* (born Lisburn, Co Antrim 1831; died Balham, London 1904). *Watercolour over pencil on white paper.*

A painting by McCloy entitled Strickland's Glen, Bangor, *owned then by J R Hall, was exhibited in 1893 in the Belfast Museum and Art Gallery as part of the "Loan Collection of Works of Art, chiefly relating to old Belfast". This is possibly a study for it. Strickland's Glen lies near Connor Park, off the* Bryansburn Road in Bangor. The basis of these tight watercolour studies is a careful pencil drawing which would be meticulously coloured in with pure transparent watercolour washes, working from light to dark. McCloy shows his particular skill, based on observation, in differentiating the dampness of the stream against the dryness of the sun-dappled rocks and foliage.

MONDAY	9	THURSDAY	12
TUESDAY	10	FRIDAY	13
WEDNESDAY	11	SATURDAY/SUNDAY	14 / 15

CITY HALL UNDER SNOW: *William Conor* (born Belfast 1881; died Belfast 1968). *Oil on canvas on board.*

This wintry view of Belfast was probably painted in the 1920s, at a time when Conor was establishing himself as the most popular and representative Belfast painter of his generation. Like many Belfast artists, he began his career as a lithographic technician or "black man" with the local poster firm of David Allan. He was a brilliant recorder of Belfast scenery and life, and though held in high popular esteem, he lived modestly and was never financially successful.

MONDAY **16**   THURSDAY **19**

TUESDAY **17**   FRIDAY **20**

WEDNESDAY **18**   SATURDAY/SUNDAY **21 / 22**

DRUMFRESKY, CUSHENDUN: *James Humbert Craig* (born Belfast 1878; died Cushendun, Co Antrim 1944). *Oil on board.*

The son of a Belfast tea merchant, Craig was practically self-taught as a painter. He established himself at Cushendun in the Glens of Antrim. With Paul Henry and Frank McKelvey, Craig must rank as one of the definitive Irish landscape painters of the inter-war years. Craig was tremendously prolific as a painter, and the Glens of Antrim, Donegal and Connemara were his favourite locations, though occasionally an English, Swiss or Spanish landscape can appear. Craig died at his beloved Cushendun and was buried there. His widow bequeathed twelve of his paintings to Bangor Borough Council which installed a Craig Room in Bangor Town Hall.

MONDAY   23   THURSDAY   26

TUESDAY   24   FRIDAY   27

WEDNESDAY   25   SATURDAY/SUNDAY   28 / 29

Christmas Day

RUINS AT HOLY ISLAND, LOUGH DERG, CO CLARE:
Bartholomew Colles Watkins (born Dublin 1833; died
Dublin 1891). *Oil on canvas.*

A regular exhibitor at the Royal Hibernian Academy from 1860, Colles Watkins devoted himself to painting Irish landscape in a particularly detailed style. Places like Connemara and Killarney featured among his favourite sites. As he worked slowly, his pictures are not plentiful. This is a very good *example showing Irish monastic ruins against an evocative sunset. On one of his sketching tours in Co Kerry, Watkins caught a chill which turned into pneumonia, from which he died.*

MONDAY **30**

THURSDAY **2**

TUESDAY **31**

FRIDAY **3**

WEDNESDAY **1**
New Year's Day

SATURDAY/SUNDAY **4 / 5**

NIGHTFALL, CONNEMARA *c.* 1962: *Maurice MacGonigal*
(born Dublin 1900; died 1979). *Oil on board.*

Maurice MacGonigal was President of the Royal Hibernian Academy and father of the art critic Ciaran MacGonigal. The artist stated that this was painted on the spot, a short distance from Roundstone, Connemara, close to the junction of the "bog road" to Clifden and the road from Roundstone to Cashel. It was late evening, in the afterlight. The painting was shown in *the Oireachas Exhibition in Dublin in the same year (1962) and bought by the Thomas Haverty Trust, who presented it to the Ulster Museum.*

Dunabad. Co. Cork

MONDAY 6

THURSDAY 9

TUESDAY 7

FRIDAY 10

WEDNESDAY 8

SATURDAY/SUNDAY 11 / 12

EVENING, MALAHIDE, CO DUBLIN *c.* 1893: *Margaret d'Arcy (active late nineteenth century). Watercolour on paper.*

This charming sketch comes from the large album presented to the painter Sidney Mary Thompson in recognition for the hard work she had carried out in organising the Belfast Art Society, the forerunner of the present day Royal Ulster Academy. The painters whose watercolours were mounted in the album came mostly from Belfast, but occasionally, as in the case of d'Arcy, *from the Dublin area. Many were amateurs, but skilled painters in spite of this. The great tradition of respectable amateur work in watercolour has been carried on in Dublin and Belfast even up to today.*

MONDAY 13 THURSDAY 16

TUESDAY 14 FRIDAY 17

WEDNESDAY 15 SATURDAY/SUNDAY 18 / 19

MOUTH OF THE SUIR: *Thomas Walmsley* (born Dublin 1763; died Bath 1806). *Watercolour and bodycolour on brown tinted paper.*

The son of an army major of Lancashire origin, stationed in Dublin, Walmsley moved to London after quarrelling with his family and friends, and worked as a scene painter at the Haymarket Theatre and Covent Garden. In 1788 he was back in Dublin painting scenery for the Crow Street Theatre. Walmsley's style involves much gouache or bodycolour slapped on with the broad bravura he would have acquired as a theatrical scene painter. His compositions and lowering skies can be very dramatic, as here, with well-placed figures. The Suir enters the sea in Waterford Harbour, and a coloured aquatint after Walmsley's style entitled Mouth of Waterford Harbour, *engraved by R & D Havell, was published by John Murphy in London, on 9 December 1809.*

MONDAY	**20**	THURSDAY	**23**
TUESDAY	**21**	FRIDAY	**24**
WEDNESDAY	**22**	SATURDAY/SUNDAY	**25 / 26**

LANDSCAPE, IRELAND *c.* 1956: *Patrick Hickey* (born India 1927). *Oil on canvas.*

Patrick Hickey qualified as an architect at University College, Dublin, in 1954. He won an Italian State Scholarship and studied etching and lithography at the Scuola del Libro, Urbino. His first one-man exhibition was held at the Dawson Gallery, Dublin in 1961, and in 1962 he founded the Graphic Studio in Dublin. He later taught architecture and engineering at University College, Dublin. This is an early work inspired by the landscape of Co Wicklow and the geometric pattern comes from the way that forestry plantations are constructed.

Acknowledgements

The publisher wishes to thank the following for permission to reproduce work in copyright:

Alicia Boyle for Potato Washers *by Alicia Boyle; Mrs M Campbell for* Claddagh Duff *by George Campbell; Tom Carr for* Twylight Moyadd *and* Mourne Foothills *by Tom Carr; Patricia Kay Dalzell for* City Hall Under Snow *and* Ferry Boats, River Lagan *by William Conor; Gerard Dillon for* Yellow Bungalow, Children Playing by the Lagan *and* Glenoe *by Gerard Dillon; T P Flanagan for* Green Landscape *by T P Flanagan; Patrick Hickey for* Landscape Ireland *by Patrick Hickey; Derek Hill for* Tory Island from Tor More *by Derek Hill; Frances Kelly-Boland for* The Window *by Frances Kelly; The Lefevre Gallery for* Dublin Street Scene *by Edward Burra; Ciaran MacGonigal for* Nightfall, Connemara *by Maurice MacGonigal; Hector McDonnell for* Bewleys Restaurant II *by Hector McDonnell; Sadie McKee for* In the Mournes *by John Luke; P Lippington for* September Evening, Ballymote *and* Coal Quay Early Morning *by Colin Middleton; Ian Stoupe for* After Milking Time *by James (Séamus) Stoupe.*

While every effort has been made to contact copyright holders, the publisher would welcome information on any oversight which may have occurred.